BE THE
BUFFALO

STEVEN DUDLEY

CONTENTS

ACKNOWLEDGMENTS

I would like to acknowledge a few people who helped me get to this point. Seth Godin, without you and the altMBA I would not have leveled up, defeated my impostor syndrome, tackled the resistance and evolved to a greater state. My Wife, without your commitment, support and intelligence this book wouldn't have been worth the paper it was printed on. Jayson Krause, the coach who initiated the change. Without the spark there would be no fire. Every interaction I have ever had has bought me to this first book, so, thank you to everyone who has played an impact in my life.

AUTHOR'S METAPHOR

A book helping aspiring entrepreneurs prepare for the peaks and valleys of the journey ahead. The entrepreneurial road is unique, and very similar to a long hike through the mountains. You embark on the journey because you enjoy the uphill challenge, you're looking for something different, a chance to get outside and create your own destiny. Finally, you do it for the personal satisfaction of reaching the top, not to prove to everyone else that you can do it but to prove it to yourself. Obviously, not forgetting that you do it for the breathtaking panoramic views.

The crazy thing is though, almost all entrepreneurs don't prepare enough for the hard part. They forget that they were looking forward to the struggle. They weren't expecting the trail to be so hard, so bumpy, so unpredictable, so unforgiving. They didn't realize how steep the incline was and most importantly they didn't foresee the weather patterns.

Most entrepreneurs understand that the trail can be hard and they can physically muscle their way through it but what makes and breaks most of them is the storm that rolls over the mountain tops every other day. That storm is what makes most entrepreneurs drop their belongings and turn around. That storm is what makes another big portion of entrepreneurs hunker down, break for shelter, look for safety and try to weather the storm.

The entrepreneurs that make a difference, build the things that matter, create massive impact, and change the world are the ones that are prepared physically for the rocky road and prepared mentally to walk into the storm and just keep moving

CHAPTER 1

INTRODUCTION

We are on a mission to provide entrepreneurs the keys to a successful journey, so they can build the things that matter. Entrepreneurs change the world, so why wouldn't we give them everything they needed to be successful and act on as many ideas as possible? Why do we put this big, audacious stigma on entrepreneurship? Why is going against the status quo frowned upon and seen as dangerous play? We are here to change that stigma and help entrepreneurs build their dreams, act on their ideas, and fight for a better future.

ENTREPRENEURS ARE THE KEY TO EVOLUTION.

Evolution in my mind is growth, forward progress, change, development, something new, a new way of thinking, a new way of getting things done, being more effective, being and doing something better than in the past. I could keep going, but I think you get the point.

Yet, it seems as though society holds entrepreneurs back. Even more than society, most successful entrepreneurs consistently say that it is the people closest to them that are their biggest haters, doubters, or obstacles.

What the hell is going on here? Why do the people we need the most create the greatest resistance? Where is the encouragement? Where is the enthusiasm and safety net for these beautiful humans? Why does society congratulate promotions and pay raises but squint, grit their teeth, and take a step back when a person who decides to take the harder, but more important role of entrepreneurship?

I will tell you why, from my perspective: I suspect they are cowards. They are sheep, who are comfortable being comfortable and can't see a different version of the future. They avoid pain at all costs and aren't willing to sacrifice safety for change. Finally, and most importantly, they don't believe what you believe.

Even though entrepreneurs encounter all of this resistance, some of us still LEAP. We leap because we believe in something. We leap because there is no better reward than seeing an idea come to life and being a part of evolution. No matter how big or small the change is, it is evolution. A micro dent in the world leads to macro dent in the world. Sometimes, it is the collaboration of multiple micro dents that cause the macro dent.

NO MATTER HOW SMALL YOUR IDEA IS, YOU ARE INITIATING AN EVOLUTIONARY SPARK.

That is why I am on a mission to make it easier for entrepreneurs to start. And not only start, but start with more clarity, more conviction and more preparation. We believe these three cornerstones will enable your business or idea get the best (and fastest!) start possible. Understanding the key elements of your entrepreneur journey before you start will save you time, money and energy. Our goal is to set you up to succeed from the start, so you are more likely to flourish in the future.

WHY? Because the entrepreneur journey is special. It does something that no other work does. It challenges you, it beats you down, it pushes you to the edge, it makes you change, and it forces you to approach things differently. It provides a well-rounded approach. In failure or in success, something happens to the brave people who take this journey. They evolve. They make change and help push this world forward.

In this short book, we are going to help you, prepare you, and encourage you to take the leap into entrepreneurship. By the end of this book you are going to say "I am ready to evolve and share my idea with the world. I am ready to face my fears, fight through them and be the buffalo (don't worry we will get to that in a minute)". More importantly you'll say "I am ready to change the world".

We will highlight some of the key trip wires on your path, prepare you for some of the general obstacles in front of most entrepreneurs and give you some of the most important tools, tricks and advice to prepare you on your journey.

What Change am I Trying to Make?

I am changing the way we prepare for entrepreneurship. I am changing the mindset of the new entrepreneur starting their first journey. I am trying to change the longevity of an entrepreneur's journey by starting the journey with purpose and clarity. I am changing the ease in which people can understand their ideas and then create them.

I am changing the way people engage and perceive struggle. From… struggles and failures are bad and I shouldn't share them… to… struggle and failure is the bridge to evolution and I must share it with the world to help others.

I am changing the way entrepreneurs prepare for the journey ahead. Helping them see that this game is not based on your physical strengths and EGO but based on your vulnerability and mental strength. The more prepared you are to be wrong, learn from your mistakes, adapt, change and evolve into something new, the more likely you are to succeed.

WHO is this For?

What defines an entrepreneur? Who am I talking to? In my definition, an entrepreneur is someone who is willing to take a step outside the box, draw outside of the lines, go against the grain, trust themselves to walk alone, challenge the status quo; someone who would do anything to create their vision or art and someone who sees a different way to do something.

As you can imagine, this applies to more than just the Silicon Valley boys and girls club that are creating apps, blockchain models and solving billion-dollar problems. They certainly do count and I love that club, but this goes much further than that. This goes to the corporate employee who has had enough of following the protocol and sees a new way of solving the same problem and so they go out of their way to develop a new strategy or approach. This is also for the corporate employee who has been looking at spreadsheet for 8 years straight and has had enough. They want to enjoy life and follow that weird dream of owning an ice cream shop because they love ice cream and they love the way it makes people feel.

This is also for the 45-year-old parent who has been hiding in the shadows, using their kids as an excuse, using their significant other as an excuse and lying to themselves for many years. You know who you are. You are incredible. You are the hardest working person I know, you know more than everyone around you because you have been sitting back patiently collecting information for so many years. You haven't had the desire, courage and energy to act, and now your time has come. The kids don't need you anymore, you're at home alone, your time is free, and your purpose for the second half of your life is about to be very powerful. It's time for you to believe in yourself, time for you to act on your needs and wants, time for you to show the world what you've got, time for you to prove to yourself that your worth far proceeds your weight. Show the world what your mind and body can do, it's your time to shine.

- CHAPTER 2 -

I AM NOT A GURU

There is a time and a place for a guru and this is neither the time or the place to call me a Guru. To be a guru, would mean I break down the barriers ahead of you and show you the way.

This is not the case with me and or anything I do.

I am here to help you struggle and show you the perspectives you may not see, so that you can survive this struggle.

I am an expert at being me. I am not an expert of being you. For that matter, no one is. Only you know the right answers and only you can make the decisions that will impact you. The only way you can find ultimate success is by doing the work yourself; do not expect anyone to do the work for you until you do it first. Dig in and do the work, make the decisions, be accountable for your actions and get ready to learn, pivot, and evolve.

I may hand you a machete or two, but it is your job to fight back the long grass.

In fact, most of this book is layered with insights that I think will be extremely helpful for entrepreneurs. The point of this book is to push you into entrepreneurship with more preparation than I had. What you need to realize very quickly as an entrepreneur is that, there are a million ways to get started. A million ways to fail. A million ways to be successful. You need to decide which information you like and don't like. Be selective in who you listen to. Don't copy everything from your favorite mentor.

Take 15 of your favorite gurus, leaders, mentors, writers, bloggers and more. Take the parts of their story you like, the parts that resonate with you and start your own story. That's what entrepreneurship is all about. Creating your own story by stitching together the ones you hear along the way.

So, when you read through this book remember I am not always right and I am not here to hold your hand. Hand holding is for kids. You are an adult. I am here to push you into the struggle (when you're ready) and be right there encouraging you to be the buffalo… (OK, OK, I am just building suspense, you'll understand the buffalo in the next chapter, I promise.)

I am not a guru, I am not a teacher. I am a coach. I am an instigator of action. I am a different perspective. I am like the ghost of Yoda who will leave you with an insight or two and laugh hysterically when you think you have figured it out. Hopefully, my words will help you think differently, push you forward, and give you enough self-belief to take massive action towards building your dreams.

- CHAPTER 3 -

BE THE BUFFALO

An interesting title for this book, no? Well, here's the story.

My wife was proofreading this book as she is my better half in every way, extremely intelligent and actually understands spelling, punctuation and grammar rules unlike myself. When she was just finishing up the reading, she said...

"You know what would be really great is if you could stitch each of the sections together with a short story, for example the story of the Buffalo."

My reply was simple;

"What's the Buffalo got to do with my book?."

She turned to me and said;

"What? You live in Colorado. Please tell me you know the story about the Buffalo"

And obviously with the strange look on my face she

8

knew that I had no idea what she was talking about. So, right then my life was changed and the book had its name.

The Buffalo to my knowledge is the only animal in the world that will turn and face the storm and start walking towards it. When they see those heavy clouds rolling over the mountains and the peaks of the west, they put their heads down and start hustling towards them.

Almost all animals, specifically land animals, either hunker down, hide or start walking away from the storm. This is because they're scared of what that storm brings. They know that storm will bring pain, suffering, struggle, frustration and much more. So, the last thing the other animals are thinking of doing is walking into it.

However, what the other animals don't realize is that there is a better way and the Buffalo has figured it out. The Buffalo has evolved and learned to endure the pain, face its fears and intentionally move towards the struggle. The buffalo discovered that by doing so, the storm will move over them quicker and the amount of frustration is minimized. It seems counterintuitive, it seems strange but when you really think about it, turning to face the storm even though it may be difficult, is the right thing to do.

And that is the perfect metaphor for the journey of the entrepreneur.

The entrepreneur goes against the grain, the entrepreneur walks into their fears, the entrepreneur wants nothing more than to engage with the storm because they know that on the other side is a clearer version of the future. Once the hard part (the storm) passes, they can be more productive and make the changes necessary for future success.

This whole book is about preparing you to be a better entrepreneur, and there is no easier way to say it other than… be the Buffalo. Turn and face your fears, walk into pain and struggle because that's where growth lies, that's how you'll get ahead of your peers and that's how you'll find the next calm before the storm.

- CHAPTER 4 -

OVERCOMING FEAR

Talking of fear and engaging with the pain: there is one fear, obstacle and struggle we all deal with. It's not what you're thinking, it's not spiders. As an entrepreneur, you now know you have to be the buffalo and walk into your fears to be successful. However, there is one fear that will always be ever present for entrepreneurs... and that's you!

The biggest obstacle you will encounter is yourself. Your fears will always be there following you in the shadows. You can knock them back, but once something new appears on your journey it will creep back up.

There is only one way to defeat your fears: committing to just doing it. Doing what? Doing the thing that's new, doing the thing that costs money, doing the thing that puts you in an uncomfortable situation, doing the thing that feels so wrong, but so right. You get it. You know. For some of you it may be filming a vlog and posting it to Facebook for everyone to comment and see. For others, it will be to ask for money for the first time. For most it will be doing the actual work and committing until the end.

Every time you feel triggered, trapped, stuck, confused, lazy, insecure, distracted or some other negative feeling – that's your fear that's holding you back. Fear of being seen and judged, fear of actually being successful and having to commit to something for once, fear of being successful and having to work harder, fear of failure, fear being judged, fear of not actually being as smart as you thought you were, fear of failing your family, fear of losing money, security and safety. I bet it is one of those, if not more. Trust me, I've seen, felt and dealt with it all.

A great way to deal with it is actually talking about it or speaking it out loud. Fear is a lot like marital problems, if you don't talk about them and bring them to the surface, they get so deep they can ruin your relationship. In this case your relationship is with your work. Next time you get stuck (which is inevitable), call out what frightens you, turn and face it and engage it. By the time you're done, you'll realize it was nothing to be scared of in the first place.

- CHAPTER 5 -

FIVE THINGS TO DO TO PREPARE FOR ENTREPRENEURSHIP

Moving from philosophical help to tactical help. Before you take any big leap, pivot or life change, you must be prepared. There is nothing bigger than the career change from corporate to entrepreneur. Starting your first full time journey into solopreneurship is like going from living on land to living at sea. Living on land is stable, predictable and you have done it since you were born, so you know what to expect. Living at sea (if you haven't before) will be completely new to you. You are going to have to learn the ropes quickly, work on your balance, prepare for constant shifts in the tide and be ready to be surrounded by sharks.

You are more likely to stay alive and keep your ship a-float if you are prepared. Here is a list of 5 things that will prepare you for the journey ahead:

1. Get your Personal Finances in Line

Before you even think about casting away you must know your numbers. If you don't already keep your finances in order then it is essential you get used to it now. As an entrepreneur, you must be on top of your finances more than ever.

Prepare Your Taxes for the Year Ahead. Know exactly how much you have paid already and if you have any outstanding taxes due. And, find a tax accountant.

Organize Your Bank Accounts. Set up your personal bank accounts so you have specific account for personal outgoings, savings and an emergency account, which you never touch (unless an emergency occurs). You will need to transfer a small sum of money to open your new business account so make sure that is set aside.

Credit Card Debt - CLEAR IT! Take the step to manage your debt; learn how much needs to be paid off each month. If you are starting in debt, you may need to think twice about quitting your job. If you can establish your first sale before quitting....that would be better. And don't tell me it's not possible, I know it is.

2. READ, Listen or Watch

The best entrepreneurs in the world are normal people. They just never stopped evolving. They absorb information, stay up to date on specific knowledge and try as hard as they can to know as much as they can without being an expert (because experts you hire). Always stay open minded to new and interesting information that contradicts your own thoughts and beliefs. READ is capitalized because the best information out there is in written form, in my opinion.

If you do not currently read then you must start. I was not an avid reader until I turned 27. I found the power of reading and it revitalized my personal growth. Without reading I would not be where I am today. There is so much gold out there to be found. Remember, everything you ever need to know has either already happened or has been written about, and it is your job to piece together a new truth with that information. You just need to find it and stitch it together to form your own unique vision.

Books to start with:
o Ray Dalio – Principles
o Simon Sinek – Start with why

o Napoleon Hill – Think and Grow Rich
o Robert Kiyosaki – Rich Dad Poor Dad
o Steven Pressfield – War of Art
o Seth Godin – Linchpin
o Austin Kleon – Steal like an Artist
o Darren Hardy – The Entrepreneur Rollercoaster
o Daniel Pink – To Sell is Human
o Carol Dweck – Mindset
o Seth Godin – This is Marketing

3. Understand WHO You Are

I started two successful companies between 2012 and 2014 and they were great…for a while. I battled and grinded trying to work both businesses at once. I was on auto pilot, aimlessly pushing forward and trying to keep the ball rolling uphill.

Since I was young, all I wanted to do was help people with health and wellness. Naturally, I told myself that story and health and wellness is what I did. What I didn't realize until 2017 is that people evolve and people change.

So, there I was, kicking and screaming, making money, trying to create a massive impact. Until I realized that I wasn't sure if I wanted any of this anymore. Not only was I burnt out, but I had changed. I wasn't the same person anymore. In fact, I didn't know who I was anymore.

That being said, my businesses grossed enough passive income for me to have complete happiness and freedom. However, what you also do not learn when you are just starting out is that there is more to life than money. Money is a virus that keeps us itching and scratching for more, but when you really look deep down, you understand that it doesn't mean SH*T in terms of your life fulfillment. (Can you tell I get passionate about following your dreams over money?)

Before you start adventuring into the jungle of entrepreneurship you MUST understand who you are first. Who you are today may not be who you were yesterday or last year. We evolve (and that's a good thing). Be firmly grounded in who you are right now so that you know where you want to go tomorrow. If you have a strong relationship with yourself you are more likely to succeed. Entrepreneurs all hit massive road blocks, stressors, obstacles, triggers, fears, etc. You must have a strong foundation to be able to battle and recover from those pain points. If you go into this journey not knowing who you are, you will fail at the first hurdle.

I learned this first hand. After I sold my two business I jumped straight into a new field. I was telling myself a new story without taking the time to understand who I was. I thought I wanted to be a medical sales guy. I'm not sure where I got this from but something stuck. I spent two months navigating the turbulence of this completely different and intense field. Long story short, I got a final interview for a 'perfect' medical sales job with the market leader and I failed the mandatory personality test.

The moral of the story is, entrepreneurship is in my blood and I am un-hirable. I didn't know where to turn and so I went out of my way to understand myself more. I took multiple courses, developed amazing new skill sets, discovered new tactics and most importantly met and learnt from some incredible mentors. By the end of my self-discovery I had evolved. The experience was life altering. It was like seeing in 20/20 vision for the first time. Without knowing it I had created the first and only entrepreneur specific self-discovery course. A course designed to help entrepreneurs have ultimate self-awareness and build the foundations of who they are. I called it Journey Map.

Journey Map deepens the roots of who you are and serves as a guide on your journey. When you hit struggles and obstacles this course will help remind you of who you are and why you are here so you can recover faster and keep moving forward. It acts like a guiding map when you start embarking on your journey. If you are interested in learning more go here...

(yourjourneymap.actsofevolution.com)

4. Understand WHAT You Want

Once you understand WHO you are, you can move onto understanding what you WANT. Similar, yet very different.

This step takes time and the process of elimination. It takes hundreds of conversations, hours of self-reflection and a lot of 'doing'; as in, applying yourself and putting yourself into many different scenarios, some in which you never would have done before. There may be many different things you want to do, but it's truly about aligning your WHO with your WHAT to find ultimate fulfillment.

Finding direction in life is hard, but the good news is, there is no such thing as FAILING. Every time you find something that isn't perfect or isn't exactly what you want, you are learning something about yourself. In life there is nothing more fulfilling, rewarding and evolutionary than discovering something about yourself. It is all about narrowing down your vision. Start with a wide scope and get more refined and focused every step of the way.

Not defining what I wanted was the cause of my unfulfillment and depression in 2017. Anyone else looking at the surface would have seen that I was successful and happy. I Built two companies, helping 1000's of people, bringing in passive income, with a great team and a reoccurring business model. But what people didn't see was the complexity underneath. The stress, the frustration, the self-doubt, the stagnation, the disappointment, the unknown direction and the lagging pain of needing more impact.

It is hard to say what exactly caused my quarter life crisis but here are a few things I can point to: I had no idea what I was doing it for, why I started in the first place, what I was searching for, and how and who I wanted to help.

So, against all popular demand, logical reasoning and financial intelligence I decided to hang up my gloves. I knew I wasn't happy and I had run down to many empty rabbit holes. It was time for me to re-find myself and understand what I wanted. So, I sold everything.

Through a compilation of resources, friends, coaches, advisors and mentors I found myself and my direction again. I put so much time and effort into it I actually complied the resources and created a course from it. Journey Map part 1 address the self, part 2 address the direction you want to go in.

How to find what you want… Take my second course, Journey Map Part II is all about discovering your WHAT. To be 100% prepared for your entrepreneurial journey go here… (yourjourneymap.actsofevolution.com)

P.S if you want a shortcut - combine what you're good at with your WHY, what the world needs and what would excite you.

5. Entrepreneur Mindset

Saving the best to last. I could write an entire book on the entrepreneurial mindset, but for now I am going to break this down into a couple of points. (P.S. The book is probably coming in 2020)

Lean into your fears – If it scares you, it means you need to do more of it. No question about it. Stare fear in the face, stand in the ring with it, let it throw you a couple punches and then fight back. If you face your fears, you will learn and grow. Being scared is sometimes exactly where you want to be.

Embrace failure – Failure is inevitable. Embrace it. The whole point of entrepreneurship is to keep searching for failure, not avoiding it. Once you lean into your fears you will probably find failure. It is hard to accept, but if you are not searching for failure, you're not making a difference. It is not until you fail that you will grow exponentially. (Side note: you have to accept your failure and learn from it to evolve. If you fail and don't accept that it's your fault, play the blame game, or simply just ignore it, then you wasted your time and didn't evolve).

Be open minded – Most entrepreneurs are stubborn.

"This is my idea and I know it will work". Guess what, if you don't accept any criticism, feedback, and or listen to any advice you will not only fail but you will fail without growing. Failure without growing is the only type of failure that is true failure. You have to listen and be open minded about other's perspectives and opinions. I am not saying you have to accept them as truth, but it is your job to welcome all knowledge and then figure out what is true or not.

Growth mindset – This one is simple: read Carol Dweck's book Mindset. In short, do things that challenge you, so you can grow. When things get harder, lean in harder. Be curious to know more about the things you don't understand.

Defeat the Lizard, Reptile or old Brain – Read Steven Pressfield's – War of Art or Seth Godin's - Linchpin. In a nut shell or Ray Dalio's - Principles – You are your own worst enemy. Until you defeat your old reptilian brain that tries to intentionally sabotage any move you make outside of your comfort zone, you will never fulfill your potential. You must fight back and do exactly what your old brain doesn't want you to do. Create or do something that can be judged.

NEVER forfeit your values or your why – particularly for money – To link back to the Step 1, back to the importance of your WHO. You must know exactly WHO you are because when hard decisions come, and they will come in abundance, you must never forfeit your core values, your why and your purpose in life. I don't care how much money you are offered. It is never worth throwing the foundations and fabric of who you are away. If you stand by your values and morals and never break them, more money (and fulfillment) will come in the long run. Be the person who stands for something and never backs down.

In conclusion this chapter is all about creating an environment for yourself so you can have the perfect start.

This chapter was to give you a tactical approach to starting your journey. I numbered it to make it clear and precise. Let's take it one step further and understand the grounding philosophy to this approach...The Three C's.

- CHAPTER 6 -

THREE C'S: CLARITY CONFIDENCE AND CONVICTION

If you want to start strong, give yourself the best opportunity to be successful and create the conditions for a fast start then you need to adopt the three C's in yourself, your direction and then your idea. Particularly in that order.

The problem with most entrepreneurs is they jump straight to their idea and become obsessed with solving the problem. It hasn't been proven (yet) but I believe that the entrepreneurial failure rate and depression rate is highly correlated with the fact that entrepreneurs jump straight to the idea and forget to lay the foundations of their success. Self-awareness.

I am focusing my efforts on giving entrepreneurs a better chance at success. What has worked for me and my clients is the three C's approach. That approach starts with the self. It is imperative that you start your journey with ultimate clarity, confidence and conviction in yourself. This is the approach of step 3 in the previous chapter. Building the foundation of who you are right now, in this very moment is extremely important if you want to get through the storm.

Being the Buffalo is recommended for people who

have the three C's in themselves. If you don't, you are testing luck and fate. The more you do that the more likely you are to have a traditional entrepreneurial breakdown. Like the one I had, like the one almost everyone has. Ask any entrepreneur about their story of when they nearly gave up and what it was due to. Guarantee they indirectly point to their self-doubts, personal issues, depression, loss of clarity and faith.

The three C's in yourself are basically a defense system to yourself and the journey's dips, bumps and slumps. Having a foundation in self-awareness is like training your mind to be ready for the road ahead. I think of the movie 'Inception' with Leonardo DiCaprio. A movie about penetrating people's minds through their dreams. In the movie you can train your brain to defend against these dream invaders to make it harder for them to alter your behaviors. Whether, this correlation makes any sense to you or not, what I am trying to say is that by being self-aware you can defend against the road blocks and obstacles that get in your way on the journey.

Your direction is next aka Step 4 from previous chapter. A clear direction is needed before you start your idea. You may ask, how can you know what direction you're going without the baseline of an idea. Well, its actually extremely easy. Right now, close your eyes and picture yourself at the end of an exhausting and challenging road. You have done it! You have reached your version of success, you have changed the world around you, you are at the very pinnacle of your field, you have everything you could ever want around you... Now explain what it is you have. Write a list, dream, define success – personally (who are you at your best), financially (what do you have), friends and family (explain what the perfect scenario is), who did you help along the way, and describe what you created. There you have it... That is the direction you should be sprinting towards.

Three C's means you can define that clearly, you build

confidence that you can accomplish it and most importantly you believe you can reach it. For an entrepreneur, this task is essential. If you find yourself walking a journey for no reason you will fail. The storm will come you will start walking towards it and you will break for shelter because you don't know what you're walking towards.

Then comes the idea. This is more complex. This has more strategy. This has a lot of planning and a lot of constant shifting. Because this book is supposed to be to the point, distinct and short I am not going to write more than a paragraph on this topic. The idea stage could be a whole book in its self.

I am going to give you some Seth Godin Magic here. To acquire the three C's in your idea you must start with your WHY – this is the root course as to why you start, why you fight on amid frustration and why you want to finish the race. Next, you must answer the powerful question what is your idea for? Then, who is your idea for? Next, how do you carry out your idea (how do you do it, how do you financially make it happen)? The, what is the outcome of your idea (what do people get, what is the change you seek to make)? And finally, what do you get out of it?

The three C's should be set and reset every month of your journey. The evolution of your idea will be constant, yourself and your direction will evolve a little slower and can be re-establish every other year. The idea, will evolve over night on some occasions and on others, a few months. Once you feel that shift in the idea you MUST re-look at building the three C's to keep on track and to keep moving towards direction.

- CHAPTER 7 -

SHINY STUFF

You will always loose the three C's at some point. At least one of them. What causes that distraction, that ambiguity, that misalignment is shiny stuff. I want you to be ready for all the shiny stuff that will try its hardest to distract you and steer you off course. This takes practice but hopefully this chapter will make you aware of it and you'll be able to catch yourself before it's too late.

Entrepreneurs are notorious for jumping without looking first. I know this because I have made this mistake many times. We (entrepreneurs) see shiny objects. We become mesmerized, even fixated and don't think about anything else but that shiny object. If we are not careful, we follow that shiny object into dark places, until we realize that we have ignored the rest of life happening around us. Even worse, we didn't even think to understand WHY that shiny stuff would be beneficial to us in the first place. Whether you are just starting as an entrepreneur, stuck, hitting the ceiling with a current project, or looking to start another adventure, it is vital that you take a moment to pause and reflect on your foundations.

We all naturally evolve, adapt, change and learn throughout our lives; however, entrepreneurs accelerate that process 2X quicker than the average Joe. When you enter the journey of entrepreneurship, you force yourself into new situations and experiences on a regular basis. You struggle more and fail more, and in return, you learn, grow, adapt, change and evolve quicker than most people. Although this is a great thing, it makes it even more important to understand, discover and keep track of who you are TODAY.

As Entrepreneurs, we are naturally willing to move into new territory, take risks, make hard decisions and ride the rollercoaster at free will. But, before you take one more step or make one more decision... Understand why you are moving forward, what you are moving towards, remember who you are, why you are on this journey, who you are on this journey for, align your decisions with the foundations of you. Reset your mindset and stay on track.

If you find yourself off track, lost, enraged, triggered, struggling, confused, stuck or worse… thinking of giving up and getting a job: STOP and take a deep dive into your foundations. This will re-align yourself with who you are and get you back on track.

As entrepreneurs it is our duty to create beautiful pieces of art and the only way to do that is to be authentic in what we create. The most powerful art that you can create comes from deep within us. When you match your work to your foundations, you will create something beautiful and meaningful. When we lose track of who we are aka when we follow the shiny stuff, we lose track of what we are creating and why. Thus, our art sucks and we lose our passion.

You will constantly be evolving and discovering more about yourself as you go deeper into your life. It is your duty to keep track of your evolution and meaning in life so you can stay engaged with your art work. Your most effective pieces of art will only come to fruition if you take the time and effort to align yourself to the foundations of YOU, your direction and your idea..

When you feel like you are in a dip, frustrated, or lost

you must re-align yourself to stay as close as you can to fulfillment, success, happiness, growth, productivity and your evolution. If you do that, all the shiny stuff that appears on your journey won't play an effect on you and wont veer you off course.

This is the perfect time to talk about the Russel H. Conwell story – Acres of Diamonds. The famous story told millions of times never gets old. A long time ago in the late 1800's a farmer with a great life, a sustainable income, a manageable business and a life to be proud of, was corrupted and thrown off course. Corrupted by the idea of more money, an easier life and quicker success. A travelling priest told the contented farmer of the diamond rush. Diamonds were making people rich very quickly and there were so many stories of these beautiful stones changing people's lives.

The story goes that the farmer was seduced by 'more' and the idea of an easier life. So, he sold his land, he sold his house, he sold his old life to reach success faster. He went off searching for years, all he found was pain, struggle, bad health and no diamonds.

With very little success, he eventually gave up, decided he wasn't a good diamond digger and long wished for his previous life back on his farm. After years he finally came home with nothing and asked for his farm back. When he approached the farm, it was lively; more cattle, lots of equipment and workers out back near the stream that passed through the land.

The Famer asked the new owner what was going on? What was all the fuss about? The new owner went on to tell the old farmer that he found shiny stuff in the stream and it just so happened that the shiny stuff was a stream full of diamonds.

There are many morals of this story but here is what I think entrepreneurs should take from this story. Stay in your lane. Don't get impatient. Don't worry about the success of others. Remember what you're doing this for and why you started. Don't get seduced by the shiny stuff because the shiny stuff is closer than you think. You are the only one who is in control of your success and you need to define if you are playing a finite game or infinite game...

- CHAPTER 8 -

INFINATE GAME

Entrepreneurship is an infinite game. Yet, most entrepreneurs see their projects in black and white, or are looking to win. These entrepreneurs are playing a finite game. Meaning they are looking to finish first, they see entrepreneurship as an ends to a means, as a short hike to the top of one mountain and when they summit its all over. These entrepreneurs may win the fight but they will lose the war. In my opinion the journey of entrepreneurship is never won, nor is it lost. Once you understand that, you will start to understand that the journey is really a series of mountains and each summit you struggle to reach gives you something more to life.

For example, a financial goal of 10 million dollars means nothing if it is accomplished easily, quickly and without struggle. That 10 million dollars will become a fleeting moment of 'oh that's cool' but then it won't be enough. It won't be enough because you didn't struggle for it, you didn't earn it, you didn't fight for it.

Lets give this example an example. The early and quick rise of the childhood star. Many to choose from so I will not single anybody out, but this success without struggle leads to a finite collapse in many cases. The childhood star expects everything to be easy from here on out and has not prepared for future struggles. They believe they have reached the top of the mountain thus, making everything from there a less meaningful.

This experience of a finite win is dangerous, it leads to bad leadership, entitlement and personal destruction. When you struggle for a win you're more prepared to reach for more, you're uneasy at the top of the mountain and you use that vantage point to look for the next mountain. Its commitment to the infinite game that is most rewarding, not having one big win.

Entrepreneurs' success should be measured in evolutionary leaps. The entrepreneur should have success every day they conquer a struggle, learn from their past and pass it onto the world.

Entrepreneurship is an infinite race you should always be looking to struggle and level up. If you're not, declare yourself out of the game once you reach your version of success and tell the world you're no longer an entrepreneur.

Knowing that this game has an end point (finite) or it's a lifetime game (infinite) gives you power over your journey. It gives you a sense of fresh air filling your lungs. You feel lighter and at peace with your journey. Not constantly fighting for the next thing. Once you commit to the infinite game you are clear to go about your days enjoying the struggle.

For some of you and I hope most of you, no matter how big or small your dream is, you have realized that living a healthy life, and enjoying each struggle, pain, gain, and excitement is what matters most. It's not always about reaching the goal, it's about enjoying the ride.

- CHAPTER 9 -

ACTUALIZE DON'T IDEALIZE

To reach your 'enough' you have to do something miraculous. You have to go from idea to action. I know it sounds crazy but you actually have to act on your thoughts.

Entrepreneurs live in the clouds. Specifically, entrepreneurs who are starting their first journey. They spend most of their time dreaming of the final vision, idealizing over their heroes, and not taking any action. The thing that sets the successful entrepreneurs from the rest – they are action takers, they are DOERS.

Changing your mindset from thinking successful entrepreneurs like Reid Hoffman, Bill Gates, Steve Jobs, Jeff Bezos and Zuckerberg are 'Gods', to instead thinking, 'they are normal human beings who had a dream and started taking steps for the dream to evolve, so they had to evolve'.

My point is, idealizing successful entrepreneurs is a waste of F**KING time. Listen to their blogs, YES. Read their stories once, SURE. Be curious about what they say, ABSOLUTELY. But don't you dare idealize, deify, or worship them. They are ordinary people who took extreme action and started to actualize their dreams and ideas. By doing that they self-actualized, reached higher, self-actualized again and so on. You can do the same thing! You

29

just have to stop putting them on a pedestal and focus on creating traction.

No one can help you grow, evolve, self-actualize more than yourself. You hold the key to your own success. When you turn 100 years old, you will want to say, "I reached my potential". The best way to do that is to keep making strides forward in the direction that you want to go in. Not the same direction as everyone else or the same direction as your idols. You are unique and to actualize you must find your own path. The path unknown is the path that will bring you most progress.

When you place yourself back to back with these other entrepreneurs, all you are doing is wasting time and setting yourself back. Stop worrying about what other people think, comparing yourself to others, looking in the past, giving yourself excuses, and listening to the resistance/lizard brain (read Linchpin or War of Art). GET OUT OF YOUR OWN WAY and just start DOING! (or making a ruckus, thanks Seth Godin).

The point is… comparing yourself with anyone else is the subject of your demise.

Take what your idols give you and run with it. No, actually, SPRINT with it. Take it as far as you can go. Once you hit a roadblock or obstacle, then you can re-visit your idols. Re-visit their work, their advice, their podcasts etc… and then pick something new up that you can sprint with again.

- CHAPTER 10 -

DREAM ONCE AND DO

I want to hammer actualize don't idealize… Here is another way to spin it. If you don't get the point I am trying to make then I'm not sure entrepreneurship is for you (strong opening statement but hopefully you really lean in here and act).

Dream once and do. Dream again and do more. Then, dream again and do more. DON'T KEEP DREAMING until you have done something about it.

The bigger the dream, the harder it is to start and the harder it is to act, the harder it is to find clarity. You get the point. If you have a massive dream, I want you to narrow it down to its simplest form so that it may become feasible. I am not saying don't dream big. I am saying dream big and then make it plausible for yourself.

Entrepreneurship is about acting on your dreams until you fail or if your lucky have so much success you can't keep up. Let's set this straight: a dreamer is someone who envisions a different version of the future and they will do anything to make it a reality. A fantasizer is someone who is picturing a future, but never actually create it.

Are you a dreamer or a fantasizer?

Dreamers ACT, dreamers DO, dreamers fight for the future they want until it becomes a reality. No matter how big your dream is you must start somewhere. A lot of people struggle with no knowing where to start: I always say, just START somewhere. Start building your dream brick by brick.

Fantasizers live in the clouds and never come down. These are the woulda, shoulda, coulda people. The people who thought about the latest and greatest gadget a year before you but did nothing about it. They let fear seep in. They let self-doubt get the best of them. They are day dreamers not dream doers.

It can be frustrating fighting for your dreams, because some days it will feel like you tried so hard and didn't get anywhere. Sometimes it will feel like your dream is so close, but still so far. Sometimes you will get to see a small replica of your dream and then it fades into the distance again. These are all tell-tale signs that you are taking action. Get excited about those frustrating moments. Change your mindset from 'urgggg so close, why can't it be easier' to 'YES, one day closer to my dream, bring on the struggle!'

I need you to promise me that your dream won't become a fantasy. Promise me you will take small, mini actions. No matter how big or small the dream is, you have to start taking mini actions. Day by day building your cathedral. Maybe someone else will finish your cathedral but at least you started it (thank you, Jayson Krause). Dream once and just start DOING.

- CHAPTER 11 -

THE POWER OF GIVERS GAIN & CONNECTIONS

One of the consequences of 'Dream Once and DO' is that you start meeting people. By doing something about your idea it means you have to talk to people. It means you have to engage in conversation and start enrolling/convincing people that your idea can help them or someone they are linked to. Sometimes 'DOING' means stepping outside of your comfort zone and talking to someone new.

At first, these conversations are going to feel uncomfortable, maybe painful and maybe even damn right awful. Regardless, you have to start somewhere and you have to actually leap. The more you fail the more it means you are growing, learning and refining your message. One conversation at a time, you will narrow your statement, conversation, or pitch down to its perfect form. But only by doing will you get it right.

Once you start to hit the nail on the head with your talking points, you will start to see this amazing thing happening. You will start to realize the power of connection. The more you engage, help people, listen to people, explain your idea to the right people, and put yourself out into the world the more you will feel as if the world is working in your favor. I highly suggest the givers gain policy as well (AKA give to people and help people without the intention of receiving anything back and naturally it will pay dividends).

You must let go of the thought process that you need something from someone in particular and so you must seek them out. Instead, replace that mental constraint with "I will make powerful connections with anybody at any time". The more powerful connections you build, the more powerful you become. The more you are willing to help, the more the world and your powerful connections are willing to help you. The world works in mysterious ways and always repays greatly, unselfish acts of intention never go unnoticed.

Try it today. Tell your story and listen to a stranger's story. Offer them help, ask if you can do something for them, or even better just do something for them without them asking. Help them connect with someone in your network. Whether it is beneficial for you or not doesn't matter. It is the power of that connection that matters. Be a leader, be a linchpin, be a giver in society, build your connections by giving, listening and helping. Watch the power of your connections slowly bring you to exactly where you want to be.

- CHAPTER 12 -

IT'S YOUR FAULT

There is something I need to tell you about choosing to be the buffalo and intentionally walking into the storm. Once you are actualizing, doing, connecting, giving, building and engaging with that storm, you will have to start accepting that from here on out everything is your fault. Yes, everything.

If you hire a marketing team, to start running ads or manage your presence, and things aren't working the way you thought, its your fault. If you bring on a client and you are doing everything you can to make a change for them but nothing is happening because they aren't doing what you said, its your fault. If you pay someone to build a website for you and it gets a poor click through rate, it's your fault.

What I am trying to say is that, whatever the situation you need to start accepting and finding the ways it's your fault. You have chosen this destiny and it is your job to own every outcome. You are the owner. You are the founder. You chose that title by becoming an entrepreneur. Now you have to take full responsibility for it.

The best thing about this mindset shift is the end result. By owning it's your fault, you have an opportunity every time something goes wrong to learn. To learn something new. To learn a new way of creating success. To learn a better way of communicating what you want. To learn a better a faster way to create impact. This list could go on for miles.

'It's your fault' is essential for entrepreneurship. The best CEO's have been doing this for years but it took them years to figure it out. However, you have the chance to start your career as a CEO embracing this mindset, putting you years ahead of your peers.

- CHAPTER 13 -

ENTREPRENEUR STRUGGLE'S

Moving onto a couple of obstacles, barriers or struggles that you will definitely come across. Entrepreneurship comes with a specific bundle of pains. Some are unique to each person but I have highlighted two that seem to pop up in 90% of all entrepreneurs' stories. I don't write about things that don't matter and these two struggles matter a lot. Dig in.

Over Complication

All entrepreneurs are not the same. They do not have the same struggles. Everyone has a different story to tell and everyone is unique. However, without a shadow of a doubt, one thing all entrepreneurs do to themselves is over complicate things.

There is so much to do, so many things to focus on, so much advice, so much, so much, so much of everything. The one thing that sets the greats from the 'I can't break through' is themselves. When the entrepreneur journey fails, it is almost always the fault of the entrepreneur. They get in their own way and they over complicate things.

If there is one thing that is different for me on this go around, it is simplification. I am finally getting out of my own way and simplifying everything I can. I am not trying to focus on 10 things at once and be average at all of them. I am trying to do 3 things at once and be great and consistent at all of them. KISS – Keep It Simple Stupid.

I know that this message is being told 100 different ways from 100 different people but they are saying it because it is true. It is so simple, yet so many entrepreneurs ignore it. Gino Wickman say's 'you have to say it 9 times before they listen'. It can't be truer in this example. There are hundreds of other ways you (entrepreneurs) can get in your own way, but don't make this one of them. Focus on three things and do them so well, so efficiently, so consistently that it doesn't even feel like work anymore. It becomes habitual and automatic. Once you master the three, then you can start adding.

The reason we try to do so much at once is because we think we can. But guess what, when you are just starting out, you can't. The best entrepreneurs in the world mastered many things but they didn't master them all at once. This is an infinite game (thanks Simon Sinek). If you are a true entrepreneur, you are not doing this to make a quick buck. You're doing this because you believe in something. You can't change the world in a year.

Clear the path ahead of you, get rid of the ambiguity, put road blocks up in front of all but three of your paths. Make it easier on yourself, not harder. Reduce the amount of work and decisions you have to make. Life is hard enough, get out of your own way and make the road to success easy. I heard Reid Hoffman say "Trust = time + consistency". So, to gain trust from your customers/ target market focus on doing three things really well. Then keep doing them really well once a day for a whole year. Stop over complicating this journey. P.S we will talk about trust in more detail a little later…

Ask yourself, 'what are the three most important things I can do that will make a difference overtime?' If you find yourself doing more, slap yourself and say not yet.

Perfectionism

Let me get started by saying that I think we are all uniquely weird and we all hold the trait (not sure if it's a trait or a learned behavior) called perfectionism. Every single one of us has little quirks, things, ways, and jobs that have to be perfect. You may be the worst dressed person in the world and you couldn't care less what you look like in public, but you just spent 60 minutes writing the most beautifully architected email in the world and its damn right perfect. You know it's true. We all have a few things that we just want to be perfect (some more than others, you know who you are). We are all pre-wired to be perfectly different and... let's face it, weird.

Now to the point, I personally believe perfectionism holds us back.

I hate perfectionism and I am trying really, really, hard to take it out of my life. I have been searching for 'good enough' lately and it is driving my wife crazy. Recently, we have been debating what the fine line of perfect is and what is good enough is vs. what is too sh*tty to throw out into the world.

Background – My wife is incredible. Unbelievably intelligent, beautifully passionate, extremely experienced and about as close to perfect as you can get. However, I think her corporate experience has destroyed the idea that 'its ok to fail and not be perfect'. Whereas, I have never held a full-time corporate job in my life, created two companies and working on a third. A rebellious entrepreneur who has unconventional intelligence, has no respect for the status quo and lives in the clouds.

The struggle – If people are judging your work constantly now a days, why would you want to put something in the world that wasn't perfect. People expect perfect so therefore you must produce perfect work. Why wouldn't you do everything in your power to create something perfect? If it's not perfect, will you be judged and discredited or will you be deemed successful and brave? Is perfectionism holding us all back from creating and sharing our work with the world? Or is it improving the level of work we produce to the world?

These are all questions and statements I don't know the factual answers too. Maybe there isn't one, but here is my opinion:

I think if you have an idea, whether it is a big idea, or just a small book like this, it doesn't matter - you have to share it with the world! I want to see that idea in any form you give me it's in. I don't care that it's not perfect. In fact, I prefer it not to be perfect because then I know it is not complete and there is more work to do. I believe that an imperfect idea is more exciting than a perfect one. Let's take this book for example. If you can read English, then you will be able to comprehend this whole piece. I am going to give it a quick scan when I am done writing and then it is being shipped out to the world. Stop reaching for perfect, searching for perfect and judging perfectly.

Start producing comprehensible work that makes a difference, changes people, pushes the line, creates impact and helps other people. That would be perfect.

I am weird, and like all of us, I am still clinging onto a little bit of perfectionism because before I started writing this piece this morning, my kitchen had to be perfect. I cannot start the day with a messy space or dirty kitchen- it has to be perfect before I start.

My wife will scold me when she reads this book. She will see mistakes and all the awful run on sentences and be annoyed that I didn't consult her before I published. But as I said, I care more about you understanding this, than I do you reading a perfectly written book. (P.S. I did end up consulting with her and having her proof read this. It was free and she is amazing. I just wanted to call myself out on this.) P.P.S This book is still far from perfect.

I guess it is up to you to figure out what is more important... To produce perfect work or for you to produce more work that just makes sense and helps people.

Fine Details

We all have strengths and weaknesses. Some of us struggle to come up with the idea or start the idea, others struggle to finish the idea or add the small details that make the idea tick. Regardless of what your struggle is, you have to point it out and find a way around it.

That is what the publication is for. To stare your struggles in the face, extinguish them with a plan and actualize your growth as a human being by telling the world how you did it.

Naming the Struggle

I will start by confidently stating that I am fantastic at drawing the big picture. I can paint a broad picture of my dreams with beautiful strokes of genius. It comes to me like Cricket came to Donald Bradman (if you don't know who this is look him up). If you need someone to see your vision and help you build your big picture, I am your guy. I will end this paragraph by stating that if you need someone adding the fine details to a painting, or someone to cross your T's and dot your I's, or if you need someone to get into the specifics of some technical details, I AM NOT YOUR GUY.

Personal journal March 2018 - I am struggling this week with the fine details of my project.

Let me paint the picture… I am launching an online course for entrepreneurs to gain massive clarity in their self-discovery before they start their first or a new idea/journey. I am launching in 4 days. The main content is complete, the website is built, the payment options are set-up, the course is operational. Here is the problem. I have to create feedback forms, I have to do a buyer persona and empathy map to understand my customer in more detail, I have to create some videos for a better user experience, I have to think about my marketing options and SEO, I need to link the course to an automated process to link the answers with the final outcome (map). All of these fine details are the death of me. They trigger me. They bring me to a place of frustration and quite frankly just piss me off. I wish someone could just finish the F***ing thing so I can move onto the next thing and get back to the big picture.

Dealing with your struggles

If I were coaching myself, I would ask myself "What are you willing to give up control of and what are you willing to do yourself". Answer is I have spent too much money putting this course together, for one last time I need to suck it up and get into the weeds. My promise to myself… I will never do something alone ever again. I will outsource my pain and weaknesses to utilize someone else's strengths from here on out.

How am I going to deal with these obstacles? Dig in. Dig in to the pain. NO PAIN, NO GAIN. If I do this now, I will know for next time what to do (and there will be a next time). If I can set it up now so that it can be 80% automated for later, I will save myself time in the long run. I will make sure on these final days, I give myself an outlet, a reward so to speak. I will make sure I complete one of my recovery tactics (that I discovered in my course) every night so I can be fresh getting through these final days.

Struggle = Evolution

How did I grow from this struggle? By pushing through these struggles, I am giving myself a learning experience. I am learning how to commit to a finished product. I am committing to seeing this project through and making sure (whether perfect or not) that I ship this out to the world. These fine detail struggles will give me confidence knowing I can hack through the weeds and life will be just fine. I have also learned for next time that this is what help is for. If someone can do something better than you, why the hell would you want to do it anyways?

Evolution of EGO. I do not have to oversee everything.

I do not have to work alone. I do not need to commit to perfect. I am imperfect and other people can provide me with help.

Evolution of resistance. 'Hey, self-doubt. Hey, self-sabotage. Hey, worry and fear... screw you. I am posting this, I am completing these final fine details and I am getting this out to the world whether you like it or not.'

- CHAPTER 14 -

DECISION MAKING: THREE DOOR CONCEPT

To be able to get over obstacles, defeat your fears, embrace the pain, struggle well, be the buffalo etc… you need to embrace decision making. Embrace that decision making is hard and the only way to get better is to learn from your mistakes. Also, that decision making becomes easier the more you do it. Also, accept that not all of your decisions will be the correct ones and you'll need to learn to move on very quickly (this is called sunk costs please refer to Seth Godin's work on this topic). You'll also learn to give yourself permission to be wrong in the first place. Finally, be prepared to take your time with any big decisions. You must be able to weigh the importance of each decision appropriately.

Entrepreneurs be prepared for decisions to come at you from all angles at an uncomfortable rate. Get used to it because it doesn't stop. Ever.

Let's talk about the three-door concept that Reid Hoffman and Jeff Bezos talk about. When a decision comes your way you must, first (very quickly) weigh the importance, secondly, you must decide if this is a one-way door, a two-way door or to ignore the door all together and keep walking the corridor.

One-way doors

One-way doors - A big no going back kind of decision. A one-way door is a decision that you can't turn back on, a decision that once made, is finite.

When you come across a very highly weighted decision, quite often there is no turning back. Once you walk through that door you must be prepared not to look back and just keep walking. When making these decisions you must accept that you can't go back. Side note, don't you dare start comparing the past to the now future, once the decision is made it's made. One-way door decisions are scary and you should take your time in deciding if you are going to walk through or not. Once the decision is made and whether you discover it was the right decision or not, you must accept it and accept any costs that come along with it.

One-way doors shouldn't be coming up too often. If they are it means you are falling into a traditional entrepreneur trap - the shiny stuff trap we talked about before. One-way doors can be hugely successful for your business, movement or idea. They can add extreme amounts of value but on the other hand, they can break you and set you back just as far.

Point being, try and peek through the gap or ask to look inside for as long as possible. Gain as much research and insight as possible to help you make the best educated guess as possible.

Two-way Doors

This is a decision that you can easily go in and out from. A decision that holds almost no penalty for making. A decision that you can pull away from just as easily as you stepped into. A decision you can make with ease, over and over again.

When you recognize one of these decisions, it is imperative

that you make it quickly, decisively and with great conviction. Decisions like these hold no great weight, so don't sit and dwell over it. Dwelling makes your life harder and slows down your progress. If the risk is low and you can get out of your decision, just go ahead and make the choice quickly with strong conviction.

How do you save time on two-way decisions? The answer: know your values, your vision, direction, and your goals.

Values: the easiest way to start making these decisions quickly is by making decisions based on your values. If you hold a strong commitment to your companies or personal values then you can easily make on the fly decisions. For example, my core values are honesty, caring, creativity, evolution and energy. If a decision makes me compromise any of my values I do not commit. Or, if the decision was making me compromise one of my values is it strengthening one of my other values so much that it is worth it?

Vision and direction: by knowing which direction and where you are headed you can ask yourself this very simple question... Does this decision help me get closer to my final destination and or at least the direction in which I want to go? IF NO don't make it, if YES then walk through that door. To have a strong sense of direction you must have a clear vision. I know vision work in the coaching world gets a bad rap and trust me coaches who spend too much time here irk me as well. Regardless, having a known end point that you are walking toward is essential for decision making. You never want to be walking in wrong direction. Side note: How will you know if you need to walk back out the door if you don't know what you're searching for in the first place.

Goals: goals are things you want to achieve that will help you get closer to your vision. Stepping stones to cross your river. Very similar to vision and direction, if you know what your goals are you can easily know if decisions will help you with your goals or not. Two-way doors are amazing for helping you achieve your goals. Because goals are mini action points you can find those two-way doors that can help you achieve those goals. I would use those decisions as an advantage. I find as many reversible decisions as possible to help you achieve those mini steps.

Two-way door decisions are essential to your business. You need to make these decisions quickly and plentifully. Ensure you don't compromise your values, ensure the door helps you with a goal and ensure that door helps you get closer to your vision. Use two-way doors to your advantage. Stick your head in, peak around, get everything you can and then, once you have received what you need, either walk back out or settle in and get the most out of the decision.

Walking past the Door(s)

I know this sounds ridiculous. Why the hell am I reading about walking past a door? Because making the decision to say NO is just as important and as valuable as saying yes. As I mentioned earlier, entrepreneurs love to say YES and get distracted by the shiny stuff. It is fact, there are whole entire books on in, it's almost a guarantee that entrepreneurs will be hypnotized by something new and sexy.

On all entrepreneur journey's there will be more than one occasion where something really big, transcendent and shiny will magically appear on your path. Almost always, especially young or new entrepreneurs will take the bait and start walking off their trail toward the mirage. Needless to say, almost always there is no nirvana, clean drinking water or lush trees at the end, just a massive waste of time and distraction from what you set out to do in the first place.

The trick is to know how to say NO and stay on your path. The nirvana is already in front of you. You had a dream at the start of this journey so don't get distracted, stay on course and walk toward that specific nirvana. The only way to be ultimately fulfilled, it is to struggle through the pain, embrace the tension, and fight to make your dream a reality.

As an entrepreneur you will always have a choice. Heck, entrepreneurship itself is a choice. When all these decisions start coming your way, you need to be able to distinguish what choices each decision comes with. Weigh the options, weigh the importance and weigh the outcomes. The more you decide, the more you will speed up the process, and the more you will recognize the mirages from the helpful stepping stones to the massive game changers. You will learn to use two-way doors to your advantage, when to take the leap with a huge decision and when to say NO and keep on walking.

- CHAPTER 15 -

YOU'RE NOT GOING ANYWHERE WITHOUT TRUST

I told you trust would come up later. As well as decision making, trust is something that is essential for entrepreneurs. Trust makes and breaks entrepreneurs. If you cannot be trusted you cannot survive. Trust is vital in every industry, it is common among every exchange of service, product or relationship. Without trust you are losing. Losing not only in your entrepreneurial journey, but your life as well. Trust is the foundation of every single exchange we have, from our family, our loved ones, our friends, and our working relationships.

What is trust? Trust is in that invisible space along with love, passion, funny feelings, spiritual belief and all the other gray areas. It is hard to define. Oxford Dictionary says, "firm belief in the reliability, truth, or ability of someone or something." So, basically, to build trust you need to change someone's belief of you. How the hell do you do that?

I heard this basic, but true equation on how to build trust:

TRUST = CONSISTENCY OVER TIME

Based on that definition, you're telling me, if you just

show up, consistently, over a period of time, you'll gain someone's trust? That is the simplicity of it. Now, you can go on to say that you need to show up in the correct demeanor, stand strong by your WHY statement, believe in something and be consistent in your values. I am assuming, as an entrepreneur, you already have a sense of that. There is nothing stopping you from building trust right now. Whatever it is you are searching for or building, it doesn't matter, just start showing up consistently, time over time again and start building your relationships.

Start showing up, start getting in the equation, in the room, in the space, in the face of the people you need to get trust from. To move them in any way you must be trusted, you must be in front of them, showing them your values, your why and your message consistently, as much as possible. Side note: don't be the fake salesman, aggressive type of person. Trust is an organic process. Trust is a foundation to relationships, so build it well, build it strong, show them your vulnerabilities and share with them your story over time.

A story of trust. No one has more trust than the great Warren Buffet. His whole entire empire is built on consistency over time. This man is the king of trust. This man oozes trust. He got his very first investment partnership based on trust. He bought his first business based on trust and the rest is history. This man shows up day after day, showing intent to learn more, being ahead of the curve, listening, watching, staying relevant, staying consistent and doing it time after time.

- CHAPTER 16 -

WHERE THE HELL AM I GOING?

We all ask this question in our heads and if you haven't yet you will. There is something about entrepreneurship that brings out our best and our worst. As entrepreneurs you will have a bunch of down days. You'll have those moments of self-doubt and question yourself, you'll say what am I doing, or where am I even going? This small chapter is to prepare you for the inevitable. We all want to know where we are going and guess what: it's impossible to know, so, GET OVER IT. You cannot plan every second of your life.

What you can do is close your eyes, imagine pulling yourself out of your body and going way up in the air so you can see your whole entire life timeline view point, start to finish (this is called metaview). Now, look straight down, you see that tiny little spec, that's you.

First, you have to understand that everything behind you is complete. It has already finished. Your past has shaped you, molded you and given you what you have to this very point in time. You can learn from the past and use it to help you make the decisions right now and in the future. What you cannot do is dwell back there, sit back there or hide back there. That is called SUNK COST. Look it up. Get over it and live right now.

Secondly, it's what you do right now that shapes the future. It's what is happening in your brain right now as you read this that matters. The power of living in the now is what brings you most fulfillment. However, sitting in the power of now to think of what you want tomorrow is completely acceptable.

Planning for Tomorrow...

Where do you want to go? Take yourself back up to your metaview: in one year from today you will be further up your timeline. What do you want that place to be on the timeline? Is it a beach/vacation is it celebrating a completed project, is it celebrating your kids' graduation, is it quitting your job and starting your new venture? Visualize it, picture it, put it on the timeline and start working towards it.

This isn't goal setting, this is dream actualization. I know the world has beaten you down and told you dreams are dreams and they can't be accomplished. I CALL B.S. You can dream, and you must. Dream hard, reach far and be fulfilled with your life. You only get one. Reach for the stars because once you name your dream it becomes real. And once it becomes real, it becomes obtainable. Once it becomes obtainable, the world will help it become reachable.

So, post it to the world. What is your 1-year dream?

If someone says it's impossible, tell them "thank you" and keep on fighting for your dreams. Only you can give up and only you can reach them everyone else can either help or go back to their unfulfilled world.

You are on a path to your dreams and only you can stop you.

"Get busy living or get busy dying" – *Red, Shawshank Redemption*

- CHAPTER 17 -

LONELINESS OF
ENTREPRENEURSHIP

Everyone says and preaches that entrepreneurship is really hard. But what they don't tell you is why it's hard. I will tell you one of the reasons it's so hard, because its lonely as heck. You alone have to deal with all the problems, fires and frustration. You alone have to deal with all the excitements, wins, and success. You alone have to learn how to do everything. You alone then have to deal with everything else in your life. There are so many peaks and valleys, loops, twists and falls that no one else would understand.

Trying to articulate just one normal day to a non-entrepreneur is a job in itself. It's exhausting. Not only that, but most of the time you're talking gibberish anyways. You end up bottling up a lot of your emotions and stories. This is not good! In fact, this is a recipe for disaster. There is only so much you can handle alone. You can't take yourself off your island, but what you can do is invite people to your island. Or, even better, you can connect a bridge between your island and other entrepreneur islands so you can share with your peers.

Creating a peer group of entrepreneurs is one of the

most powerful things I ever did. I can't tell you how good it feels to be in a room full of your peers who feel the same things you feel, who are dealing with the same pains you are dealing with, who share the same challenges and understand the same concepts. When you can relax in a group of people and let everything off your chest – now that it is an empowering feeling.

The road is lonely and you must be strong. However, you can defend against it. You can prepare for it and you don't have to be plagued by it for years, like I was. Sharing is caring. Your peers need to hear your stories and you need to hear theirs. That way you both know, you are not alone.

- CHAPTER 18 -

BENEFITS OF FAILURE

Before I wrap this up, I wanted to give myself one last stab at reframing your mindset. The title for this chapter could be 'Benefits of being the Buffalo'. Another essential for entrepreneurs is to realize the power of failure and truly nestle into the fact that failure is always a good thing. The only way you can truly fail is to fall down and not learn why you fell and not want to get back up. Your perception of failure has to change. If you constantly try your hardest to fail there is nothing but success waiting for you. Easier said than done but here are five benefits of failure:

Clarity: Disaster creates clarity. When everything falls down, you can see the things you couldn't with all the obstacles and obstructions in your way before.

Resilience: Once you get knocked down, you learn how to fall well, you learn how to recover, you learn why you failed and you become stronger for it. It's like your immune system, you get stronger every time you get sick and your body learns how to defend against it next time.

Humility: You are not perfect. You can get hurt, you can get better, you can be stronger, but you don't know everything. When you fail, you become a little less invincible and that's a good thing, because it inspires a new round of growth.

Creativity: In order to achieve success, you must fail. When you fail you have to think in a new way, see new perspectives, construct new avenues and be more creative to get over the hurdles that tripped you up last time.

Real Relationships: Your weak relationships will become clear once you fail, because they will fall off the band wagon and disappear into the night. Your strong relationships will become more relevant and stronger.

"Success consists of going from failure to failure without loss of enthusiasm" — *Winston Churchill*

- CHAPTER 19 -

THOUGHTS OF AN ENTREPRENEUR

A conclusion but not an end. Whatever anyone ever says, the road of an entrepreneur is the most beautiful road in the world. I don't care how much pain or failure I encounter, there is nothing better in life knowing that I created something that made a difference, helped someone, and made a small part of the world a better place for future generations.

I believe that to create ultimate fulfillment or self-actualization, we must all be a part of something similar to an entrepreneur's journey. For the reason that experiencing, struggling, and learning is the best and quickest way to grow (personal evolution). When we personally grow, we have a better chance of becoming our best self and our best self can create the things that matter. Our best self can build something to help with your own or someone else's struggle, and that is the best way to start a project (idea evolution). Finally, showing the world what you learned, how you struggled and what you created helps others with their struggles (world evolution).

But to create that sort of evolution, you have to go against the grain, do something almost no one else is doing, be willing to walk into pain, struggle and failure because you know when you get through the storm you come out stronger. You need to be the buffalo.

Experience + Struggle + Learn + Create + Help = Evolution

I encourage you to give more than you take on your journey through life and find a way to leave this world a better place for the next generation.

Evolution of YOU
Evolution of your DIRECTION
Evolution of your IDEA
Evolution of the world

ABOUT THE AUTHOR

Steven Dudley has never held a full-time job. At 22 he made a decision to take his clients from the big corporate gym and work for himself. From that decision came two incredible health and wellness businesses over 7 years. A corporate wellness service covering 3 states, 15 locations and impacting 1000's of employees. As well as, a high-end luxury wellness service for two of the most affluent condo buildings in Denver, CO.

After experiencing the highs and lows of entrepreneurship, Steven discovered that fulfillment and personal development was more important than financial stability. So, he sold the companies and started taking a deeper look at who he was, what impact he wanted to make and how he could leave this world a better place for future generations.

Steven is now the founder of Acts of Evolution LLC an entrepreneur development ecosystem. Developer and creator of the Journey Map experience. A Two-part online course helping entrepreneurs accelerate their personal evolution and getting them closer to building their perfect business. Creator of the Idea Incubator - the only forum-based idea development program. A master entrepreneur coach with experience on hundreds of projects, 1000's of people helped, and hours of conversations pushing entrepreneurs to walk into the storm